# Wild Gardens

# Wild Gardens

Poems by

Sara Letourneau

© 2024 Sara Letourneau. All rights reserved.
This material may not be reproduced in any form, published,
reprinted, recorded, performed, broadcast,
rewritten, or redistributed without
the explicit permission of Sara Letourneau.
All such actions are strictly prohibited by law.

Cover design by Shay Culligan
Cover image by Mike Sleeper
Author photo by Kristie Dean

ISBN: 978-1-63980-552-5

Kelsay Books
502 South 1040 East, A-119
American Fork, Utah 84003
Kelsaybooks.com

For Jim,
like nobody ever

# Acknowledgments

Heartfelt gratitude goes out to the following publications where these poems or earlier versions of them first appeared:

*Amethyst Review:* "Gifts," "How to Color a Mandala," "How to Pack for Iceland," "Hraunfossar," "The Triptych and I"
*ArLiJo (Arlington Literary Journal):* "The Spider," "A Strange Easter," "Twilight in April"
*Aromatica Poetica:* "A Drop of Frankincense Oil Speaks" (as "Self-Portrait as a Drop of Frankincense Oil"), "An Ode to Icelandic Tap Water," "Peach Pie Ice Cream Haibun"
*The Aurorean:* "Glimpse of a Bald Eagle," "Hunter's Moon," "Late Winter Cardinal," "Twilight in April"
*The Avocet:* "Fog Rolling In from Oyster Pond," "Growing Tomatoes"
*Blue Institute:* "Lament of the North Atlantic Right Whale"
*The Bookends Review:* "Head of the Table"
*Boston Area Small Press and Poetry Scene:* "A Strange Easter"
*Canary:* "Osprey at Bass River"
*Constellations:* "2:00 A.M.," "An Ode to a Tibetan Singing Bowl"
*Curry Arts Journal:* "Eve of Spring"
*Didcot Writers:* "Beyond"
*From the Farther Shore: Discovering Cape Cod & the Islands Through Poetry*: "At the Sandwich Glass Museum"
*Full Mood Mag:* "No Darkness Here (An Ode to Metal Music)"
*Golden Walkman Magazine:* "No Darkness Here (An Ode to Metal Music)"
*Living Crue:* "In the Bath," "Self-Portrait of the Poet, Looking at a Photo of Herself"
Mass Poetry's *Hard Work of Hope:* "Flowers at a Funeral"
Mass Poetry's *Poem of the Moment:* "An Origin Story of Cape Cod" (as "Cape Cod: A Geological Origin Story")
*Muddy River Poetry Review:* "Breath of a Humpback Whale," "Gas Station Valentine"

*Nixes Mate Review:* "Elegy for Snaefellsjökull Glacier"
*Offerings: A Spiritual Poetry Anthology from Tiferet Journal*:
    "Self-Preservation During a Pandemic"
*Soul-Lit:* "At World's End," "Elegy," "Learning to Be," "Moose Hill Street Lullaby," "Wild Gardens (Ars Poetica)"
*Underground Voices:* "Naked Truth"
*The Weekly Avocet:* "Great Egret in Central Park"

*  *  *

"Krýsuvík" received 11th place in the 2023 *Writer's Digest* 17th Annual Poetry Awards.

"Lament of the North Atlantic Right Whale" won the Poetry category in Blue Institute's 2020 Words on Water Contest.

"Naked Truth" is also anthologized in *From the UV Files,* the 2012 best-of anthology from *Underground Voices*.

"Variations on a Tornado on Cape Cod" was featured during the Plymouth Poetry Forum's 2023 Independence Day Poetry Marathon on Facebook.

If I've learned anything from my experiences as a poet, book editor, and writing coach, it's that it takes a village to publish a book, no matter the genre. So to all of the following people, thank you from the bottom of my heart.

To Carmen Barefield, Brittany Capozzi, Amanda Davis, Shannon Kelly, and Michael Rosati, for your feedback on early versions of many of the included poems—and, more importantly, for your friendship.

To Nadia Colburn, Vievee Francis, Beth Knaus, Oliver de la Paz, G.G. Silverman, Donna Baier Stein, David Walker, and Ran Walker, whose workshops inspired some of the poems in this collection.

To Wayne-Daniel Berard, Elya Braden, Rob Colman, Karen D'Amato, Dr. David A. Fedo, Risa Fowler (aka Cit Ananda), Joe Fusco, Jr., Erica Jacobs Green, Mary Beth Hines, John Holgerson, Allan Hunter, Sandy Kaye, Alice Kociemba, Deborah Leipziger, David P. Miller, Nadifa Mohamed, Brian Mosher, Rebecca Hart Olander, Gabriela Pereira, Eliza Reid, Robin Smith-Johnson, Paul Szlosek, Ron Whittle, and Rich Youmans, for the guidance, support, encouragement, and inspiration each of you offered at different points in my writing career.

When I work on poetry, I listen to music that helps me focus on or become immersed in the memories, imagery, or mood of what I want to write. So without the songs and music of these artists, this collection wouldn't be what it is today: Adele, Anathema, Atoma, Bebo Best, Christopher Lloyd Clarke, Donna DeLory, Michael Brant DeMaria, Early Cross, Ludovico Einaudi, Brian Eno, Flowing Tears, Dan Gibson, Hugar, Jessita Reyes and Yoga Tribe, Friðrik Karlsson, Katatonia, Arjen Lucassen and Guilt Machine, Sarah MacLachlan, Jeremy Soule, David Walker, Jack Wall, and Within Temptation.

To my family, for your love and for encouraging my writing ever since I was young.

And to Jim, for making my life as full as it now is, for wanting to see this book become a reality as much as I wanted it to, for telling me to never stop writing (and creating that handy spreadsheet to keep track of all the poems), and for being who you are. I love you so much I can't stand it.

In 2017, I attended the Iceland Writer's Retreat for the first time. The experience inspired some of the poems in this collection and brought me back to poetry after a four-year break. This was made possible by the enthusiasm and generous GoFundMe donations from these people: A.S. Akkalon, Sam Bader, Dan Berkman, Justin Boyer, Brittany Capozzi, Kendell Clark, Jeri and Rick Coffey, Jaclyn Cucinotta, Glenn Cunningham, Shay Emory, Molly Enrick, Charlie Farrell, Cindy Harnden, Emily Hayse, S.J. Higbee, Keith Hubbard, Ariel Hudnall, Helena Jean-Louis, Suzanne Jette, Sandy Jordan, Shannon Kelly, Shirley and Bob Letourneau, Sara Litchfield, Katie Moynahan, Jessica Matteliano, Bethany Mazza and Peter Letourneau, Jody Moore, Paul O'Neill, Jim Pappas, Michael Rosati, Jeff Ross, Leanne Sowul, Andi Toli, Victoria Grace Tucker, and Larry and Noel Walsh.

# Contents

## One

| | |
|---|---|
| An Origin Story of Cape Cod | 19 |
| How to Pack for Iceland | 21 |
| Great Egret in Central Park | 22 |
| The Triptych and I | 23 |
| No Darkness Here (An Ode to Metal Music) | 25 |
| Eve of Spring | 27 |
| At the Sandwich Glass Museum | 28 |
| How to Color a Mandala | 30 |
| Riding a Horse in Iceland | 31 |
| Wild Gardens (Ars Poetica) | 33 |
| Twilight in April | 34 |

## Two

| | |
|---|---|
| Self-Portrait of the Poet, Looking at a Photo of Herself | 37 |
| Breath of a Humpback Whale | 39 |
| Krýsuvík | 40 |
| Head of the Table | 41 |
| A Strange Easter | 43 |
| Hydrangea Blossoms | 45 |
| Hraunfossar | 47 |
| Peach Pie Ice Cream Haibun | 48 |
| In the Bath | 49 |
| Beyond | 51 |
| Gas Station Valentine | 52 |
| Flowers at a Funeral | 53 |

## Three

| | |
|---|---|
| Elegy | 57 |
| Osprey at Bass River | 59 |
| An Ode to a Tibetan Singing Bowl | 61 |
| 2:00 A.M. | 63 |
| Learning to Be | 64 |
| Locked-In | 66 |
| Variations on a Tornado on Cape Cod | 67 |
| Hunter's Moon | 71 |
| Late Winter Cardinal | 72 |
| Self-Preservation During a Pandemic | 73 |
| Naked Truth | 75 |
| Fog Rolling In from Oyster Pond | 77 |

## Four

| | |
|---|---|
| Growing Tomatoes | 81 |
| Elegy for Snaefellsjökull Glacier | 82 |
| A Drop of Frankincense Oil Speaks | 84 |
| Moose Hill Street Lullaby | 86 |
| Lament of the North Atlantic Right Whale | 87 |
| The Spider | 89 |
| Glimpse of a Bald Eagle | 91 |
| Letter to Mother Earth During a Severe Drought | 92 |
| An Ode to Icelandic Tap Water | 94 |
| Gifts | 96 |

## Five

| | |
|---|---|
| At World's End | 99 |

One

# An Origin Story of Cape Cod

Let's start at the beginning,
twenty-three thousand years ago.
Your parents were the earth and Laurentide,
an ice sheet stretching from the Arctic Ocean
all the way to what would later be known
as the islands of Nantucket and Martha's Vineyard.
If anyone had borne witness, they would have found
a cold crust of white as far as the eye could see.

This didn't happen all at once, of course.
Patience is both virtue and necessary evil
when you need about five centuries to emerge.
But not once did you complain as, leisurely,
your more glacial parent retreated north.
In three lobes, it scraped over bedrock,
carving and molding you into moraines, kames,
and outwash plains as if with a sculptor's tools
but no final design in mind.

In its wake, it strewed all manner
of rock debris over you—miles upon miles
of till, gravel, sand, and boulders hundreds of feet thick.
But you didn't mind. You liked the way
the meltwater streams dressed you, how their deposits
filled your deltas and expanded west,
how leftover lumps of ice melted
and made jewellike kettle holes along your peninsula.
You even chose to bear your relict valleys,
your riverless battle scars, with pride.

You couldn't fathom then
that, one day, you'd be robed in
pitch pines, marshes, and cranberry bogs
or called home by piping plovers, seals, and humans.

You didn't even care about your name until
the Wampanoag and the Nauset called you Turtle Island
and the British colonists Cape Cod.
No. That long ago, your only care
was that you were born,
and to be born means to exist,
and to exist means boundless possibilities.

# How to Pack for Iceland

Leave the umbrella at home.
The wind there has a will of its own,
and you might not want to tempt it.

Plan to dress in layers.
How else can one prepare
for the unpredictable?

Waterproof your body
in duck down and feathers
and a tortoiseshell of nylon.

Your feet will want hearths as well,
so give them shoes to keep them warm and dry,
with cushioned midsoles for support.

Don't forget the usual necessities:
your passport, your phone, a granola bar,
a change of clothes in your carry-on.

Most importantly,
make room for the things
you won't expect to bring home:

fistfuls of fresh air, wild and pristine,
deep breaths of black sand and lava salt,
the music of geysers and vast countryside,

rhapsodic rivers and vacillating sky,
singing themselves into your belongings and
spreading like incense smoke once the suitcase is open.

Last but not least, take a selfie before departure
so you can compare it with the one you take
upon your return.

# Great Egret in Central Park

They say one should expect
the unexpected in New York City.
Perhaps they mean the subway violinists,
the assailant pigeons, or the lost dollar bills
sprouting out of asphalt.
But no one ever said to expect you,
the white duchess of wading birds.

I admit, the grackles, those iridescent
black-and-blue thieves, don't surprise me.
Nor do the mallards and the wood thrushes.
Yet here you are, treading the edge of the pond
as if it's a path you've walked thousands of times.
Your black spindle legs draw step after careful step.
Your sinuous neck angles low as you scan the water,
head poised with the knife of your bill.

Could you teach me how to fish
with your stillwater patience?
Or how to stand so motionless
that my limbs turn into cattails?
How is it that you and your self-assured stroll
have become the center of my morning?

Moments ago, car horns were baying,
jackhammers clattering, and the five million
footsteps falling citywide a constant hum.
Now there is only you and me and a countryside quiet
that reminds me of the weed I found last night,
green and growing through a crack in the sidewalk.

Do you mind if I sit here a little while longer,
just to watch the miracle that is you?

# The Triptych and I

When you look at a landscape photograph,
what do you see?
Most likely the scene itself,
all wildlife and weather and time of day—
and certainly not the soul's terrain.
That was what I had believed before
the triptych caught my eye and bade me stop
at the gallery's front door,
its panorama of a Cape Cod sunset
bathing clouds and beach in pastel violet-blue
and tugging at an anchor under my ribs.

Before I knew it,
I had drifted across the threshold
like a dinghy whose moorings had come loose.
Maybe I still would have noticed the triptych
if it had been a single, larger whole.
But at that moment,
those three acrylic panels
hanging side by side
displayed not just sand and twilight,
but an evening that I swore
was my self-portrait.

I was the setting sun, radiating
light that was all my own
yet hiding from view.
I was the ocean tide, reaching
for land despite the moon's backward pull.
I was the beachcomber
roaming the shore, gathering seashells
yet knowing I had already found
what I was looking for.

I was silver and emberglow,
cerulean and rose, horizon and cosmos,
all the things I wished I had seen in myself sooner.

I didn't take the triptych home with me.
Nor did I ask for its title or the photographer's name.
Instead, I carried the memory out the door
like a tangling in the throat
when you feel understood even though
you haven't spoken a single word.

# No Darkness Here (An Ode to Metal Music)

One chord,
and I plunge back
into the nights when I would steep myself in you
and your whorling of riffs and double-kicks,
syncopated rhythms in waltz or quintuple time,
sometimes bathed in synths and strings,
sometimes led by soprano seraphim or baritone kings
and other times by beasts of nightmare.

I never simply listened.
Each of your songs was an ocean,
and I would submerge myself, drifting underwater
until your perpetual canon of voices ran slick across my skin
and the opening notes thrummed with the final ones
like the convergence of two seas,
and only when I surfaced would I remember
that I was supposed to be analyzing you,
critiquing you for a magazine's audience.

Fast-forward to tonight—
you still call to me as if by name,
even though last night my amygdala craved
Adele and Lindsey Stirling,
but metal is a wolf's cry,
howling not just to the dark corners of my soul
but to the whole moon of it,
craters and shadows and light and all,
and so when you beckon in the echoes
of Katatonia, Ayreon, or Within Temptation,
I can't refuse.

Yes, you know me,
down to my most explosive truths,
such as how some metalheads don sundresses
and flip-flops instead of corsets or all black,
or how some rebels speak compassion
so they can keep their revolution for the pen and page,
or how there is no darkness here
but an ever-expanding universe full of
cascading solos for comets, crescendos for supernovas,
nebulae of dust and self, hydrogen and—
dare I say it?—
beauty.

One chord,
and I plunge back
into the ocean you made for me,
back into a body of music you made
with my own flesh and bone and tissues,
with a cadence akin
to a heartbeat.

# Eve of Spring

Spring begins tomorrow.
You'd think it had already arrived after
a winter of little snow or cold.
I didn't notice; this year,
winter raged in my soul.
Loss of friends, death of a loved one—
they brought winds that cut through my bones
and summoned tears.
I stayed indoors, having no desire
to reach out to others
yet yearning to be reached.
What a waste of time and life.
Self-pity, I've learned, only means more suffering
the longer you let it snow on you.
So I will end this season now.
When I wake in the morning, even if the hurt
lingers, I will run out the door
with every inch of me open
to greet the sun.
I will stop to lean down
and comb the earth with my fingers
and smell its dampness.
I will find the nearest gazebo
and visit it again during a rainstorm,
so I can watch nature's madness at work.
And I will smile at more strangers
and bid them hello. Everyone longs
to be acknowledged like the first flower of March—
as if they're coming home,
as if their presence matters to at least
one living person.
So do I, and that will happen
once the season changes outside and within.

# At the Sandwich Glass Museum

Every hour, on the hour, the glassblower
dons his protective sleeve and readies his tools
at the museum's furnace, a freestanding brick pillar
that could be mistaken for a chimney.
In front of a crowd of thirty, a class from the local
elementary school, he introduces himself,
explains where the glass nuggets come from
and what he's going to make, but not how he'll make it.
The students and teacher nod, rapt despite
sweat beading on their foreheads.
After all, they're here to learn the "how."

He takes the pipe, one end immersed
in the furnace's 2,000-degree heat, and reaches
deeper inside to the crucible of molten glass.
Out he draws his first gather, pearlike and comet-white,
kept on center by his constant spinning of the pipe,
his fingers turning the rod as deftly
as a spinner spinning wool into yarn.
He blows a breath through the pipe's cool end,
trapping air inside the glass so it inflates,
then sits at his bench and shapes the swell
with the closed blades of his jacks
so it's smooth and symmetrical.

Back and forth, the glassblower moves
from the glory hole to reheat the glass;
to his bench, where he sculpts it
with his jacks and a water-soaked block,
sparks flying like fireflies, steam rising from the contact;
to his feet again, to blow more breath
into his incandescent bulb,

or to "let it run," pointing the pipe downward
so gravity can elongate the honey-lava
with its bare, unseen hands,
and once to coat it in cobalt-blue frit.
His movements mimic a dancer's:
fluid, deliberate, expertly timed, choreographed
over years of training in this ancient, Syrian-invented craft.

Eventually, at his bench, he uses his shears to cut,
jacks to ply, and tweezers the size of kitchen tongs
to twist and tease the glass into its final form.
And in these climactic movements,
history comes full-circle, each motion paying tribute
to Deming Jarves, the Boston & Sandwich Glass Company,
and all the master craftsmen who brought their delicate,
igneous art with them from as far away
as England and Ireland.

All of these lessons are reinforced
in the museum's exhibits and glassware collections.
Yet none of them will draw the same delighted gasps
from the audience as the glassblower's newest creation:
a whelk shell veined in blue, so lifelike
it could have been plucked from Town Neck Beach,
just over a mile away.

# How to Color a Mandala

Who ever said
that coloring is only for children?
When you open the book to the next empty mandala,
you may think that you're looking at
a ring of exquisite geometry, or that you must
pick precisely the right colored pencil to start with.
If you're not careful, the beginning
of the process may petrify you:
thirty-something colors, just as many areas to fill,
the accuracy with which your final product should resemble
a sun, a flower, any round object that's real.
But in this moment, *should* is better off erased.
So banish your mind from the table
and let that quiet, confident voice speak instead.
Let it tell you the name of the first color,
the second color, and every one thereafter.
Think of this mandala as your version
of clay on a potter's wheel, something you can mold
with your hands and instincts.
Let the core be silver or chartreuse.
Let the outermost whorls be vermilion flames
streaked with gold, or ocean waves of navy
capped with turquoise.
Create the rules as you create—
or make none at all—
and stray outside the lines now and then.
Be as lavender, sienna, or ultramarine as you wish.
Inhale the sacred smell of your paints or crayons,
and know that you are illustrating the circle of life,
the most ancient circle of all.
When you're done, tap the shoulder
of your seven-year-old self and show them
your masterpiece, then tell your adult friends
that whoever said coloring is only for children
should try it for themselves.

# Riding a Horse in Iceland

You have to trust the horse.
It will know what to do as you ride.
The instructor doesn't say this,
but the way she mimics how to sit in the saddle
and her gentle hints as she describes
the differences between a trot and a tölt
say just as much. I take her advice
and dress myself in it, along with the rented helmet
and boots, the gloves I borrowed from a friend,
and my courage. I might not be afraid of horses,
but learning how to ride one at age thirty-four
can still pitch your heart into your throat.

Outside, the horses wait for us,
calm, almost sleepy in the early April chill.
I learn my new friend's name: Afrodíta,
a piebald beauty standing five feet tall—
three inches shorter than me—
when holding her head high,
her winter fur molting off in patches.
"She can be a bit headstrong," the instructor warns.
"She likes to ride ahead of the others."
But the horse shows no sign of impatience
as I stroke her mane and back. Instead,
she embraces me, bending her neck
so I'm between her shoulder and her head.
She even remains calm as I struggle
to swing my leg around to sit astride her,
as I correct my posture and my grip on the reins,
as I hang back so we're in the middle of the pack
when we walk out of the pen.

"Am I ready to be at the front?" I ask myself.
Soon enough, Afrodíta answers for me,
weaving around our companions
and striding into the lead, the bounce of her body
and the muscles in her abdomen shaking me,
shifting my center of gravity. My chest clenches
at her quiet insistence, but I don't question it
now that I see what she wants me to see:
the lava fields that are both maze and playground.
Every step up, down, and around on our tour,
she gestures with her head as if to tell me,

"Look at the towers of rock around us,
crusted with basaltic black but brick-red underneath.
Look at the lichen, that velvet chartreuse;
the grass, dry and long as hair,
shining gold in the daylight;
the islands of snow
and the ponds they create when they melt.
Look at the mountains that meet the sky
to the north, south, and east,
and the pillars of hotels and church steeples to the west.
Can you believe you're still in Reykjavík?
And look at the steep rise in our path,
narrowed by boulders,
and how the world opens wide as we crest it.
Do you see how your face glows
from the cool wind, the defiant sun,
and the taste of adventure?
Do you see it?"

"Yes, Afrodíta," I whisper,
breathless from the pace, the views,
and the truth in the instructor's advice.
"Yes, I see it all."

# Wild Gardens (Ars Poetica)

I hold ideas for poems like seeds in my hand,
and there are thousands of them
waiting for the brush of the breeze,
their invitation to come out and play.
Of their own volition, they leap
out of my palm into the air and land
where they choose in the open meadow.
These seeds all appear the same at first—
smooth, round, black and brown,
shining from the tender touch of morning light—
until they each take root
and grow of their own accord.
Each one knows the shape it desires—
an ocean of moss and ferns,
a tree with a thundercloud canopy,
a shrub resembling a beehive,
or a burst of daylilies—
and I've learned that none of them
take kindly to premature guidance
from pruning shears and shovels.
Instead, I let each garden become a wilderness
until it tells me the time has come.
Softer than birdsong, louder than a chorus,
each one will whisper in my ear
how it wishes to be sculpted,
how it wants to be watered and fed.
And while I am the caretaker of these gardens,
I am not the only gardener,
because they all nourish me as I nurture them,
speaking to me in petals, pine needles, and exhalations
as they guide me through each step
of their maturation process and teach me
how I, too, can grow.

# Twilight in April

The pond
is on fire tonight.

The shadows
swallowing
oaks and pines
into dusk
are such a radiant black
that they almost gleam
gold.

Vermilions
serenade
ambers, indigos,
and lavenders.

And though the clouds
are wisping,
the water
resting,
and the birdsongs
diminishing,

the world has reached
a coda—

a reminder
that it is always waking,
always rousing,
and perhaps
too candescent
to know how to sleep.

Two

# Self-Portrait of the Poet, Looking at a Photo of Herself

*Logan Airport, Boston, Massachusetts*
*September 2021*

Look at my eyes
and how they sparkle like tumbled aventurine
behind my glasses. Everyone says my eyes
are the first thing they notice about me.
So did my boyfriend when we finally sat down
to talk about love. He still swears my irises
are the color of polished nickel.
I disagree, but I won't deny that,
when in just the right light
and at just the right angle, they glow—
soft and steady, like the headlamps
we'll both wear at the Lava Tunnel cave tour
in a few days. But right here, right now,
I'm at the airport, waiting with him
for our check-in desk to open,
glasses sweetly tilted as I look at his camera,
dark brown hair half-up, half falling out
of the matching elastic; one hand tugging down
my magenta COVID mask so I can smile
for the photo (and for him),
the other hand curled around the small of my back
to reveal a peek of the opal promise ring
he gave me five months ago.
No pimples or chin hairs are visible,
the freckles on my face too small to see
from this short distance, but it's clear
from the heart-blush on my cheeks
and the vastness of my grin
that I'm thinking about the upcoming trip
and not my perceived imperfections.

Behind me, the waiting area at Terminal E is dim,
the announcement screens and white numbers
at each closed desk blurred, almost impossible to read,
as the girl in the mint green shirt—
the girl who is me—
reflects all of the room's light
like the snow I'll see atop Snaefellsjökull in one week.
Or perhaps I'm not reflecting light
but emitting my own,
a beacon of my world and his,
using lenses made of intuition that flash a message—
*Look at me, I am beautiful*—
that I'm only now beginning to believe.

# Breath of a Humpback Whale

Listen.
What do you hear
when the humpback breathes?
Of course, you know the exhalation,
that soft, moist explosion like a wave
breaking upon the shore.
But what about the inhalation?
The sound which the naturalist
who's narrating the whale watch said
is her favorite in the world,
and we should keep our ears open for it?

Yes, I know.
I can't concentrate, either.
I, too, want to watch the whale
and see the smooth slope of her glistening back,
her glacier body gliding, cutting the surface
before she dives down again and lifts her tail flukes
to reveal the white prints of her name.
And so many sounds are competing for our attention:
the chatter of the other passengers,
the susurrus of the ocean, the whipping of the wind,
the rocking of the boat. But sometimes
to hear the new and unfamiliar,
you have to do as the naturalist said
and cast your awareness out over the water
toward the horizon.

There.
Do you hear it?
Long, and low, and fathomless,
as if the whale is drinking from silence,
as if a brontide is rumbling from the deep,
as if the earth is drawing a gasp of wonder
that some of us, like you and I,
still remember how to listen.

# Krýsuvík

Did you remember, when you were there,
that five months earlier, I had shown you
photos from my visit? When you drove through
the Blue Mountains, did you feel the gravity of
my life-ghost drawing you closer?
Did the steep angle of the ascent
and the jostling from the black-gravel road
tug on your fears as they had on mine?
Did you notice how Kleifarvatn,
the lake without rivers, followed you for miles?
And when you arrived at the thermals, did you smell it—
that wall of sulfur and rotten eggs so potent
that you staggered backward a few steps?
Was the soil still painted
in gradations of rust, ocher, and goldenrod?
Was the trail veering to the right still roped off?
Did the mud pools bubble their hello?
And did you answer with yours?
Did you follow the echoes of my footprints
along the wooden walkway and up the hillside,
like you did along the streets of downtown Reykjavík,
and wonder if I had seen what you were seeing?
Did you know that snow and ice still limned
these paths in April? Did you look down
into the boiling water of the largest hot spring
and catch a trace of my reflection from when
I had stood in that spot, with my back to the railing,
snapping a selfie? Did you, at the highest point,
gaze out across the mountains and relish
the same feeling of infinity, the same
weightlessness? Did you know then
that you loved me?

# Head of the Table

"What do we do now?" my mother asks,
sitting where my grandmother used to sit
at the kitchen table. Her siblings have joined her,
their four chairs cardinal points
on a newly restored compass.
They think that we, the six grandchildren,
can't hear them now that they have sent us
to the living room to play Clue and watch the Red Sox.
But their voices are approaching thunder
to our listening hearts, which are soft and unripened
even though we have lost before
and our ages range from sixteen to thirty.

It doesn't help that none of us are speaking.
Maybe the TV play-by-play has lulled us
into nine innings of respite.
Or maybe my brother and four cousins
are still caught in last night's riptide, just as I am.
Eighteen hours have passed, but I could swear
the words "She's gone, she's at peace" have just left
my father's mouth, and the wise little girl inside me
has only begun crying and reminding him
of what she already knows:
There's nothing peaceful about
funerals, and wills, and last goodbyes.
There's nothing peaceful about the husk of you
that's left when grief shucks you dry.
There's nothing peaceful about looking out the window
at a world unchanged and indifferent to
this familial seismic shift.

But this time, it's not death that quakes me.
Cancer rarely kills by stealth anymore.
This time, it's the ashfall voices in the other room
and the knowledge of where their speakers sit.
This time, it's the unspoken inheritance
that will come in twenty, thirty years,
when my brother and I will find ourselves
in our own kitchen chairs, asking the same question
my mother asked today and accepting crowns
that will have already begun to flicker.

# A Strange Easter

*April 2020*

It's Easter Sunday, and I'm alone
in my dining room, Skyping with my parents
and my brother over orange juice, black tea,
and raisin bran with strawberries.
It's nothing like the homemade carrot muffins
or German apple pancake we'd eat together
in Mom and Dad's breakfast room during Easters past,
when it was safe for us to visit.
But this year, safe means washing hands constantly,
covering one's mouth and nose in public,
and standing six feet away from each other.
This year, in the time of COVID-19, safe means
staying home, seventy miles away from my family.

Our conversation goes as usual:
"How are you doing?"
"I'm feeling well. You?"
"Same here."
The rest is nothing new, either:
Mom and Dad's projects around the house,
my brother's upcoming (virtual) closing on his condo,
my freelance editing work,
the first daffodils to bloom in our yards.
Yet this semblance of routine is punctuated
by reminders of life upheaved:
"Did you wear your face mask at the grocery store?"
"We'll leave takeout for you by the garage door."
"Will we get to celebrate Mother's Day together?"

And all the while, I wonder if I lied.
I may be feeling well, but my longing to reach
through the laptop screen and hug my father,

kiss my mother, and riffle my brother's hair
pulls like a sore muscle. Before I know it,
the past rolls off my tongue:
"Remember when we were kids
and we'd come downstairs on Easter morning
and read the Easter Bunny's message, spelled out
in fridge magnets, then hunt for the exact number
of chocolate eggs mentioned in that note?"

My brother chuckles, says, "Yeah, I remember that."
So do Mom and Dad, and the reminiscing resumes.
And for a moment, the holiday returns to its jovial,
pastel self. Yes, it's a strange Easter,
the distance between me and them hasn't changed,
but we're together in our mirth,
together in our remembrances,
together in the tender ache for what was
and our gratitude for what still is.

# Hydrangea Blossoms

This morning, my mother clipped
two hydrangea blossoms for me,
each one from a separate bush.
She did this not on my request,
but because she had asked,
"Would you like to take
some hydrangeas home?"
Her blue eyes were blooming
the way her plants burst forth with flowers;
and as the question left her lips,
it watered me as if with her handheld hose.
"Yes," the little girl inside me spoke
with a grown woman's voice,
because a wound of disappointment
was festering in my chest,
and my mother is the kind of mother
whose body clenches with pain
whenever she sees her children cry,
no matter how old they are.

So I followed my mother
to the front yard, pointed out
which blossoms were waving at me
with their bold, bright heads.
Without question, she snipped them
with her scissors, gave them to me
with her gardener's hands
and a face creased with hope.
Back inside, she moistened a paper towel
with water at the kitchen sink
and laid it on a sheet of aluminum foil
to wrap around the blossoms' stems
for the seventy-mile drive home.

I held the bouquet again,
and it dawned on me
that one blossom was
the radiant pink of sunrise,
the other a deep twilit purple.
And for a moment, my fragile heart
broke open with such fullness,
because my mother had given me
a handful of sky—
and isn't that what a mother does?
Gifting her children the ordinary
and the extraordinary all at once?

# Hraunfossar

*Húsafell, Iceland*

What happens when you see a waterfall?
Do you reach out to let its mist land on your skin?
Shout of its magnificence to the other tourists?
Or do you do nothing because of
what stirs inside and is beyond your control?
This "lava falls," as it's known in Icelandic,
greeted me like a friend moments ago
when I stepped off the bus,
its salutation crashing like cymbals
yet hushed and rain-steady.
Now I follow the black-soil path,
reach the bend where the cliff overlooks the river,
and a swell dams my throat.
This waterfall is not like others;
not a tall, singular cascade,
but a long, sprawling multitude,
hundreds of rivulets seeping out of the lava field
into the rapids below.
On and on it flows, and I stand before it,
heart overflowing, because suddenly
I'm not here on the cliff but across the river,
where the porous rock and the glacial melt
are washing my body to the marrow,
scrubbing me clean of hurts I had borne across an ocean,
and my hands and fingers have spread
into the ledges from which those waters leap
and carry the toxins and dead cells of self away.
How do you respond then, when the world
becomes both healer and teacher?
Do you return to a sheltered, stagnant life after this?
Or do you simply go on like the waterfall,
always moving, always whispering,
always persevering?

# Peach Pie Ice Cream Haibun

It's two days after Thanksgiving, and my tongue salivates for something sweet: not a warmed piece of leftover apple or pumpkin pie dolloped with whipped cream, not the chocolate cookies with a swirl of melted Andes mint candy on top, but your peach pie ice cream. I only have to reach into the freezer and tug off the container's cold purple lid to find this cache. My hands move independent from the rest of my body, grasping the ice cream scoop and gathering a meal's worth of frozen pale orange freckled with brown graham cracker crust. Spoonful after spoonful come bursts of summer sunshine and love at its ripest. Peaches and cream cheese, sweetness and tang, velvet and cool and complete with the soft crumble of crust and the sparkle of cinnamon. And in the thick of this indulgence, I imagine you in your kitchen, pouring the chilled fruit-and-liquid mixture into the ice cream maker. I wasn't there the day you made this batch, but I had helped with the previous failure that used your old recipe and curdled on the stove, and we couldn't stop sampling the cut peaches macerating in sugar and their own juices. And I still remember my first lick of this success after it had set, how you scooped and filled a ramekin for me, how I moaned in that delighted, childlike way as its flavors bloomed in my mouth, how you smiled and kissed my nose and then my lips, and I know now

the aftertaste and
the nostalgia are not what
I will savor most.

## In the Bath

Here,
in the hotel bathtub,
I am resting
in water scented with
coconut shampoo
and arctic thyme bath salts,
rinsing myself
in solitude,
a river of reveling.
My boyfriend has already
washed my hair
and my body,
but that is not
why I feel
cleaner
and newborn.

Here,
in this bathtub,
I marvel at myself
for the first time as an adult.
Smooth, uncalloused feet
with toenails painted
the purple of orchids.
The thighs I've called
thick and flabby,
now weightless.
My stomach,
softly sloping,
a meadow of skin
inclining toward
the hills of my breasts.

Slender arms,
with hands that hold love
and fingers that give back.
Now they wave
from side to side,
creating gentle tides
that slap against porcelain,
splashing my face,
rippling, whispering.

Here,
in the bathtub,
I let my body rise
to the surface,
let my old fetal self
unfurl my limbs and neck
so my new eyes
and freshened mind
can see me as I glisten,
as I glow.
Here,
a dam I never knew
I had built
bursts inside,
and thoughts of
blemishes,
scars, and
spidering veins
are swept out to sea
as I caress
this precious vessel
that carries me.

# Beyond

What does it mean to travel beyond?
Does one need to soar past the moon, the sun,
toward the outer reaches of the universe?
Should one look farther than the blurring boundaries
between here and there, life and death, love and hate?
Or do I simply need to look into your eyes—
the pupils dark and star-spangled as the night sky,
the irises warm and brown as earth,
bursting with seeds of hopes not yet sown
but already taking root in my mind,
the gloss and wetness that aren't tears
but a doorway of liquid emotions.
I didn't know what love was, didn't dare to believe
it could step into my life the way you step over the threshold.
But when you asked if it was possible
for me to cradle your heart in my right hand
and for you to hold my left, the world beneath my feet
stilled as air and horizon spun around me,
and the word yes had never been so easy
and yet impossible to give. Now, here in this nest
we've created with our arms, you face me and I you,
and suddenly I see how we've become each other's suns,
our lives the planets that circle each other
on paths resembling a magician's linking rings—
or maybe we're riding the same orbit
now that our galaxies have collided.
Whatever the case, I know what I see,
and I welcome the tidal pull of our embrace.
How did I fall into this love?
How can time stretch so long and yet run away from us?
Does it even matter what beyond may be
when I'm already there, exploring it with you?

# Gas Station Valentine

It need not happen on February fourteenth.
Nor need it be delivered with a dozen red roses,

a box of chocolates, or a diamond necklace.
It should, however, be proof that compassion

can bloom in places we think can't be watered.
A gas station, for instance, where the stench seeps

into your clothes like secondhand smoke
and the dollars you spend siphon off your self-worth.

A space so acrid and unclean, so rich with exhaust
and morosity, that there couldn't possibly be room for

such a burst of tenderness, a small act of humanity.
Yet there it is, next to the pump's keypad—

a Post-it Note, radiant in yellow, with a message
written in black ink and smooth, careful print—

and for a moment, all the odor and commotion
of the world fall away, and all you're aware of

are those five simple, unanticipated words,
words that blink back at you like your reflection

in glass and direct your gaze inward to the truth,
words that peel you open like spring on flower buds,

words that you know you should tell yourself more often:
*You are beautiful. Happy V-Day.*

# Flowers at a Funeral

I don't want to think about the flowers.
They burn my eyes, blazing like suns
against the white parish walls
and the casket's dark polished wood.

Acknowledging them feels like whispering
profanities in this crowded holy room where
the man lying in repose is my best friend's father.
So I do my best to look elsewhere—

at my friend, whose face I cannot see as she sits
in the front row, a slight wilt to her spine;
at the pastor standing at the pulpit, one arm outstretched
as he speaks of death and the flowering cherry trees outside;

at the other mourners lining the rows ahead of me,
arranged almost as neatly as transplants in a garden—
then at my hands, the knuckles dry and cracked
from the change in seasons, as I fumble for

thoughts that are fitting for a funeral,
such as how the man I'm honoring once invited
his daughter and me to his backyard swimming pool;
and why an only child of divorced parents

must lose her father before her thirtieth birthday;
and how Death has been insatiable this week,
disguising himself as news anchors to tell me the names
of those he took through shootings, fires, old age;

and whether it's time to ask my mother and father
about their will and their power of attorney;
and how the sky this morning
is as blue as that hydrangea bouquet—

See? Somehow grief fails to blind me
to the lilies as orange as monarch wings,
the roses flushing amber and pink,
and the crepuscular rays of daffodils.

Their full blooms are faces, beatific and wise;
their stems and leaves like bodies and arms
thrown open, and completely, to the world.
They shouldn't be so thriving

on this wind-bitten April day,
yet perhaps I should give thanks that they are.

# Three

# Elegy

*Written one month after the 2013 Boston Marathon bombing*

I want to go back to the place
where millions come and go every day
but runners cross the finish line only once a year,
a public square where churches of stone
stand beside towers of glass and steel
on a patchwork quilt of grass, flowers,
wrought-iron stitching, and a brick border.

I want to go back to the street I've walked myriad times
to visit the neighbors Emerson and Grub,
to find the loosened bricks I've tripped over before,
and to finally fulfill an overdue wish
of sitting in the library courtyard
with a journal or laptop
and be my true writer self for hours.

But even more so, I want to turn left instead of right
at the intersection of Dartmouth and Boylston
and find the desecration site
where blood stained the sidewalks and screams rang out
louder than explosions.

I want to stand there and wade in what was,
throb with their pain,
taste the salt and sulfur of their tears,
hold their heads against my chest
because as long as they heard someone's heartbeat,
they were alive.

I want to drink that afternoon through my tree roots
and cry in front of hundreds of strangers,
for this city as its people bled
and, like the neighbors and first responders
and other TV viewers, I bled as well,
because our arteries were still whole
but theirs had been severed,
because we still had two legs and two arms
but they did not.

I want to go to that place,
stare at the cement and asphalt,
and reflect, and pray,
and know that eventually
windows will be replaced,
sidewalks repaved,
and bodies and memories,
though burdened with aches and scars,
will heal as their spirits flit around skyscrapers
and one another, reminding us all
that no one ever suffers alone.

# Osprey at Bass River

Look at how it stands tall at its nest,
a watchful sentry, quiet until
it opens its black, hooked beak and chirps
its kettle-whistle call. When it alights,
the thrash of its wings is palpable,
a heartbeat in my ear.

And look how it flies!
With its brown wings bowed,
its primary feathers splayed like fingers,
its white crown and vest on proud display.
Its golden eyes fix upon
the water below before it hovers,
briefly but patiently,
then dives cliff-steep, feet first,
shattering the surface with a splash.

And as it rows itself upright,
climbs into the air with a fish in its talons,
its poise does not falter
and the tempo of its flight,
a keen and vicious pulse, does not slow.
This hunt, this knowing that something
is about to die, should make me flinch,
and yet the act is so graceful,
so flawless, that I cannot look away.

How does such a thing exist?
A raptor that is wilder than a dream
does not frighten me, but rather
swoops into view and snatches my breath
the way it would snatch its prey.

Then again, the world is
bursting with contradiction.
Darkness cannot be without light,
love without hate, death without life.
And here is this king of the river,
this artful thief,
taking what it needs to survive
and leaving a gift in its wake.

# An Ode to a Tibetan Singing Bowl

No one knows real music
until they've heard you sing.
A gentle tap on your golden rim
sends a clarion call through the room,
but the concert truly begins when I run
the mallet around that thin circumference,
and your pulses vibrate from your copper alloy
through my skin and into my fingers.
Funny how you don't have to part your lips
to make a sound. Your mouth is already
wide open, and the voice streaming out
is a century-old sanctuary of shivers.

Some people say you sound like a bell.
I disagree. You sing deeper than
a mezzo-soprano, holding your quivering notes
longer than humanly possible
until they seep into muscle and bone,
and then I'm not simply listening to you
but rather immersed in you, the blood in my veins
a river of your tremors so that you become the mallet
and I your vessel, and together we soar
as a symphony of sound and sensation,
a drowsy harmony that radiates from my cells
to the tips of my toes and the crown of my head.

Have I told you how one of your sisters
once cured me of a nuisance cough?
I almost had to leave a meeting because water
wouldn't ease the irritation in my throat,
and then the facilitator struck her bowl
once . . . twice . . . three times,
and the cough faded out.

Did you know that every time you finish,
I feel as though I've woken
from a full night's sleep
even though I was awake the entire time?
Or perhaps your song hasn't ended yet
and, now that I see the air more clearly
and breathe the world more deeply,
mine has only just begun.

# 2:00 A.M.

No, the alarm clock hasn't crowed yet.
It won't for another four hours.
You've already laid there for just as long,
your head a gauntlet run of fears.

Thinking *what will happen at work tomorrow?*
becomes *how can I manage two jobs?*,
becomes *should I cancel my plans this weekend?*,
becomes *did I lock my front door before bed?*,

and all the thinking and becoming
amplifies the night until the silence snarls
like wolves and tangled hair, and the creak
of the radiator sends you bolting upright,

and the darkness blinds you, compressing you,
and your face grows numb to the shield of your hands
even though you smell the lingering notes
of lavender lotion, and even that fails to soothe you,

and that small failure sneers at you,
taunting and lying to you until
you feel not like a child but an orphan,
screaming soundlessly into nothingness

because even pillows and sheets can be
nothingness, and on nights like these
time can be nothingness, because heaven knows
you've shut your eyes and watched

phosphenes slither behind your lids
for hours, and then you roll over and find
2:07 A.M. staring at you, and you weep because
time should heal wounds, not reopen them anew.

# Learning to Be

My yoga teacher lights her candles,
one for every chakra color.
I watch them from my mat
as I do every Monday night,
sitting lotus but not yet still.
Work was a machine again today,
and though my body left the office whole,
my mind is still scattered
like beads from a broken bracelet,
and the rest of me trembles
in its rush to collect them.

She invites us now to start with Anjali Mudra—
hands pressed together over heart—
and set an intention.
My fingertips shudder like lightning,
and my breath shallows, but I try:
*I want to be calm.*
*I want to be at peace.*

And then we move, from tabletop to cat-cow,
downward dog to forward fold.
At first, my balance wavers,
the whispers in my head taunt and heckle,
and I fall behind.
Should I look up to watch my teacher?
Try to mimic how she glides from pose to pose
like a cloud shifting shape overhead
even though I will only fail?

No. I have to trust this body.
It's the only one I'll ever have.

I rise to Warrior II.
My posture, I know, is stooped,
my shoulders so high that they almost touch my ears.
But I recognize, exhale,
and adjust, and soon enough
the roots in my feet grow deeper,
my arms lengthen into branches,
and for the first time tonight
my abdomen, not my mind, is my center,
firm and engaged like the tree trunk it should be.

Gradually, every motion becomes instinct.
Every waking of my back, every twist of my torso,
every lift of my legs and opening of my chest
brings me back to Earth yet sweeps me skyward
until I am no longer a woman mired in anxiety,
but a cobra, a dolphin, an eagle, a sphinx.

Until I lie down for savasana, and there I find the truth:
I am calm, I am at peace, not because I want to be,
but because I choose to be.

# Locked-In

*For RCS*

Her eyes have opened
for the first time in three days.
Her eyes follow the tip of a finger
up and down, but not side to side.
Her eyes mirror the words
her lips can no longer form to speak.
Her eyes hover the way her hands used to
above a patient's body for Reiki.

No one in her family wants to leave
her hospital room, even for a meal.
No one is prepared to utter the words
*stroke* or *locked-in syndrome.*
No one dares to believe this healer
will never perform another miracle.
No one knows what else to do,
since she never wrote down her final wishes.

She recognizes their voices,
flicks her eyes up and down to confirm it.
She recognizes their faces
but cannot call out, or whisper, their names.
She recognizes the words they say
and the gravity of her circumstances.
She recognizes the sharpness of pain
but cannot cry out in agony.

All they can do is wait as tubes
and catheters work as her organs.
All she can do is listen to conversations,
chairs scraping, machines beeping.
All she can do is feel the touch of her family's hands
and the love underneath.
All she can do is wait
until her body tells her it's time.

# Variations on a Tornado on Cape Cod

Breaking news from the Channel 5 meteorologist
on July 23, 2019: "A tornado has been spotted
on the ground in Yarmouth, Massachusetts."

*

This is not Kansas, Texas, or Oklahoma.
When thunderstorms race through here,
their winds don't rotate.
Warm, humid air doesn't collide
with the cold and dry.
The only alleys in town
are the narrow lawns between houses,
the paved gaps behind strip malls,
the driving lanes in public parking lots.
Here, you won't find plots of grass
and wheat fields squared by roads.
This is a seaside town,
with dense marshes, pitch pines,
black oaks, beaches of bone-colored sand—
and, on any late July day, tourists.

*

I text my mother:
"Are you and Dad okay?
There's a confirmed tornado
on the ground in South Yarmouth.
Please go to the basement
or someplace safe.
Text me when you can.
I love you."

*

Outside, the sky is the same green-gray
as a storm-ravaged ocean.
Trees waver the way kelp does underwater.
A fusillade of rain—
or is it hail?—
beats on roofs and windows.
You know you should run into a closet,
your cellar, some interior room.
But you can't,
not when the whole world is rumbling,
not when the whole world is drowning.

*

I text my father:
"Hi Dad.
Are you and Mom okay?
I texted Mom but haven't heard back yet.
I heard about the tornado in your town.
Please reply or call me
as soon as you can.
Love you both."

*

Minute pass. No answer.
Their silence thrums through me, electric and violent.
The mind is now a vortex, the heart rate a tempest.
The red and green pixelated whorls on the forecaster's radar
are a sickening play on Christmas, and I think,
*I'm not ready for my first holiday*
*without them.*

\*

That evening, the gathered video footage
reveals this:
Trees ripped out by their roots
or cleaved down the middle and contorted,
limbs hyperextended.
Boats moored in the harbor, colliding
like untethered bumper cars.
The roof of a local motel peeled clean off,
exposing the rooms and occupants below.
A waterspout as white as fog
spinning its way up Bass River.
Streets near the regional high school
where some houses are victims of nature's logging
and their neighbors are barely touched.

\*

Ten minutes after my last text message,
Mom calls me.
The tremor in her voice,
the exhalation in her words, "We're okay"—
this is what will whisper me to sleep tonight.

\*

Remarkably, no one is killed.
Remarkably, no reported injuries.
"Things could have been much worse,"
some people say. "We were lucky."
True, but did you know

that as the warmth you and I keep creating
keeps transforming our world,
days like these could happen again?
That days like these could be much worse?

      *

A new episode of *Storm Stories*
airs on The Weather Channel.
Its first segment shows the 2014 EF4 twins
of Pilger, Nebraska—
siblings of ash-gray that razed
granaries, schools, banks, and homes.
My knuckles whiten as I grasp my phone
even though three weeks have passed
since the Cape's EF1 triplets touched down,
and as the voiceover continues, I almost ask the narrator:
What would you do if that were your hometown?
What would you do if, at one moment,
the whole world was exploding,
and then all that was left were splinters and dust?

# Hunter's Moon

There she is again, her face a medallion
as yellow as the halo of a tiger's pupils,

while the lithe fingers of clouds glide across,
a hand obscuring her cratered cheek from view.

Some say she's playing hide and seek, a lonely,
ancient child of the universe seeking a companion.

Others claim she's a celestial witch, she's casting
her end-of-October spell, she's not to be trusted.

Somewhere nearby, a child calls to her mother to pluck
the coin from the sky before the ghost snatches it away.

I smile and study my subject again, perceiving
her every side, her myriad myths and refractions.

She is not one character but many, a teasing Scorpio,
cool and luminescent, clutching her secrets

in the vapor of her arms, veiling her wisdom
behind brocade tapestries of dark indigo

but allowing glimpses, once in a while,
through her enigmatic expression.

How many thinkers have found clarity in her fullness?
How many lost souls have found home in her light?

Me? I sometimes see myself in her, which means
either I am part satellite or she is part human.

## Late Winter Cardinal

Winter, you must think I'm a fool.
You with all your sameness,
your listless whites and sleepy grays,
have let loose the cruelest of blessings—
a blink of scarlet feathers against the snow.

It can't be anything else,
not with its plumage as red as holly berries,
not with that familiar bob in its flight,
a quickstep in mid-air set to a tune unheard
but so deeply felt that my every reflex springs.
If I could, right now, I would chase the bird
down the snow-laced street and glide in time
with its wing-song.

They say there's nothing unusual about
sighting cardinals here in the early days of March.
But this one flies like a tremolo
erupting out of quiet, and the first splash
of morning sun has painted its body aflame.

Ah, winter, do you still believe me a fool?
Or did you choose this cardinal
as your messenger, a blazing harbinger
of the flowers yet to sing,
the sweet smells yet to dance,
the music of the earth that's soon to wake?

# Self-Preservation During a Pandemic

Two months in, I watched
the TV news reports for the last time.
By then, my worry over contracting COVID
was like an ocean churning in a hurricane,
a weight pressing against my chest
and holding me down in bed.
Each morning, I would struggle
to turn off the alarm
and function as if life were the same
even as we were all implored to isolate indoors.

The grim-faced news anchors
weren't much help, either.
Whenever they told me how many people
tested positive, I would ask,
"How many others tested negative?"
And whenever they shared how high
the death toll had climbed, I would whisper,
"How many of us are still alive?"
They never answered, of course;
never listened to me through the thin sheet of glass
that separated us, instead feeding me
facts and figures and other sober details
that tasted of nausea and fear.

I started listening, instead,
to what I knew would bring me peace,
like my heartbeat before a flow of yoga each morning,
poetry podcasts as a side dish to breakfast,
or flute and synthesizer music—
and sometimes birds—
while working from home.

I even heard the soft but deafening voice
in my solar plexus that would scream *no*
whenever someone said,
"But it's good to stay informed,
to know how bad it's getting out there."
*I'm staying informed,* the core of me would say,
since the small dose of headlines
and the next day's weather forecast
were all I could digest.

Had I chosen ignorance?
Was I pretending that all the illness and death,
all the loss and sirens and gasping
were flashes from a nightmare?
I hope not—
I was only doing
the one thing I could think of
to grab hold of calm amidst the chaos,
to quell the roiling in my head
and let my body sleep
so it could hear what it needed to hear.

# Naked Truth

"High school teacher charged with possession of child porn"

The headline screams at me,
and so does the teacher's name.
I shake my head, forsaken
by speech but not by thought.
How could they mistake
this gentle, charismatic man I knew
for a pervert?

Memories surface through the questions—
his classroom, his wire-rimmed glasses
and neatly pressed tie, the effortless,
ebullient way he'd wake
twenty-seven apathetic minds
with the glint of a book's hidden treasure.

We grew trees in Brooklyn
and danced in Capulet's ballroom with him.
We wrote sonnets and found traces
of ourselves in fictional characters because of him.
He taught me to write without thinking
and to think without wavering—
two morals I still do my best to follow.

But what of his morals?
Was there an impulse behind his smile?
At home, would he find company
in photographs of twelve-year-old girls
who were barely flourishing?
Did he find more satisfaction in studying
his own daughter than sleeping
in the bedspace next to his wife?

What I thought I knew
and what I wish not to know
have collided—a frontal boundary
of knowledge provoking a storm in me.
I see its eye, but if I look at it,
I have to accept the words I read.
And I must—it's his final lesson:

No one is ever who they seem to be.

# Fog Rolling In from Oyster Pond

Now it creeps in
from the pond toward the shore
so leisurely that it eludes the naked eye.
Only ten minutes ago, it posed
a faint and silvery threat
as it hovered above the gentle waves
and the marina's empty boats.

Now it crawls across the abandoned beach,
slithering at a patient pace, swallowing
each crumb of the coastal terrain:
the water's edge, the grains of sand,
the thick heads of marsh grass,
the vacant parking lot and outhouse,
the weathered and food-stained picnic tables,
the neatly trimmed rose bushes and hydrangea,
and finally Queen Anne Road
and the intrepid cars on her tongue.

Now this elbow of land
is a wraith, a turbid shroud
that's whiter than the great egrets
who mate here in the summer,
so pale yet so bright that you might swear
a swarm of ghosts is approaching,
then lose your footing and your breath.

Now you cannot help
but gaze at the softly blinding wall,
cannot help but marvel at
how the sky has lowered itself to the earth,
how its teeth of mist don't bite
but rather graze your skin in cool, sweet beads,

how the embrace of its milky arms is more tender
than the smothering you expected,
how you subscribe to sightlessness for a moment
so you can say you've touched the clouds.

# Four

# Growing Tomatoes

You don't need a green thumb.
At least, that's what your mother told you.
"It's easy," she said. "All you have to do
is make sure it gets enough sun and water."

But how does one quantify *enough?*
Lucky guesses don't absorb through a plant's roots
the way nutrients do. And when orchids,
fuchsias, and kalanchoe have died in your care,

you tend to question your ability to nourish others.
But fear can be an unexpected nurturer.
It can compel you to step outside every day,
no matter the early hour or the searing summer heat,

then rotate the pot so a new set of branches faces east,
touch the leaves as if they're open palms
to inspect them for hornworms or rot,
and whisper to the stem like an old friend.

How else would you learn that finding each new
starburst blossom could suffuse you with warmth?
Or that cutting Velcro strips to guide the plant
up its stake could make you, too, stand taller?

Or that watching this gangly summer-child drink
from its earthspace could sate your own thirst?
Not all of the flowers will fulfill their promise.
If most of them shrivel and fall, don't despair.

Without those failures, you would never hear
the orchestra in your heart crescendoing when
each tiny globe finally appears, then swells
to the size of a blueberry, a grape, an apricot,

and then blushes from unripe jade to yellow,
to sunrise-sky, and, at last, to sweet, succulent scarlet.

# Elegy for Snaefellsjökull Glacier

*Snaefellsnes Peninsula, Iceland*
*September 2021*

You will likely die before I die.
I was not thinking of this when I was standing in
the black-gravel pull-off along Route 574,
pressing the smartphone camera's button every few seconds
in case the previous photo was blurry.
In that moment, you were making an appearance,
cooperating with the cloudless late-summer sky
and shifting your volcano's lenticular scarf to the right
so I could see you. White as an Arctic fox in winter,
your body of ice was dense and seemingly stationary.
Later, upon checking my photos, I discovered that
your beautiful crevasses and river-waves—
the details I'd seen with the naked eye
and hoped to capture by zooming in—
were almost invisible. Instead,
the black necks of lava rock protruding from your summit
bade me not to look away.
Those rocks are ill omens, I've since been told.
They were first sighted nine years ago
because you are melting.

There is no end I can conceive for myself
that can equal the agony of yours:
dissolving from the fluid, frozen state
you reveled in for 700,000 years,
down to the sickly four square miles that's left,
growing thinner and thinner until
you're too frail to flow,
while watching your sisters in Iceland and beyond
disintegrate in the same way.

All the while, you're sitting with the creeping knowledge
that the world will one day be an enormous jökulhlaup—
those glacial dam bursts you know so well—
swallowing shorelines,
flooding coastal houses and businesses,
displacing and drowning their residents,
depriving us of the many gifts
you and your siblings share with us,
like irrigation and fertile soil for our crops,
freshwater for our thirst,
cold air to balance our climate.

I wish I could hold you out of comfort,
tell you that the future might not be so bad.
But what would make your passing worse:
The lie to ease your pain?
Or the tender, well-intended gesture?
The warmth I create—not with my heart,
but with my hands, my car, my electricity—
is only bringing your eviction date closer.
I am thirty-seven years old,
and if the estimates hold true,
you will likely die before I die, and now I know
that the rivulets and waterfalls I spotted
while driving along your peninsula's coast
are not meltwater,
but the tear-streams of a grandmother,
crying her last.

# A Drop of Frankincense Oil Speaks

At first glance, I look like a pool of water
in the palm of your hand.
I don't smell like water, of course,
but that's your first thought nonetheless.
After all, I am liquid, pale gold and so lightweight
that you barely feel me against your skin.
And no, I am not incensed that you keep staring.
Your eyes will eventually close,
and then it will be my turn to watch
as your nostrils contract and expand
and to feel the pull of your breath
against my fluid self. And then you,
by inhaling my scent, will see me anew—
not as a drop of oil, but as a garden
where the earth is sun-warmed and dew-kissed,
where pine and cinnamon trees grow on one side
and spindles of rosemary on the other,
where bonfires are burning nearby
and a bottle of balsamic vinegar is opened—
or perhaps you'll catch a glimpse of me
in resin form, when I resemble rock sugar
but can be chewed like gum
or burned to purify the air with my heady sharpness—
or maybe you'll catch a flashback
from my wild child days,
when bark from the Boswellia tree was scraped off
and my siblings and I rushed
to the surface of our mother's skin,
flowing until we formed stalactites,
sticky, redolent, unaware
that we'd soon be harvested.

And maybe then you'll remember
I am not only fragrance for your wrists
or a drop of calm you rub into your temples
or the soles of your feet.
I am also a descendant
of one of the three precious gifts
the three wise men gave to Mary, Joseph, and baby Jesus.
And while I cannot tell you
whether I can wake up your first chakra,
relieve you of stress,
or strengthen your immune system,
I'll always tell you this much:
Sometimes looking means living
through all five of your senses.

## Moose Hill Street Lullaby

Am I awake or dreaming? Some days, it's hard
to know when I'm driving down this street.

Winding, serpentine, for two-and-a-half miles it leads me
away from Route 95's choke hold of traffic as I commute to work.

This morning is one such morning. It's been three weeks
since I last slept a full night, and in these early days of autumn

the falling maple seeds remind me of the nature of my thoughts,
tailspinning but never crashing because the earth retreats

farther and farther away. It's a violent vigilance, this anxiety,
yet so deceptively quiet that no one knows I'm suffering

unless I tell them so. But the trees on this street, their leaves
barely touched by the ocher of September—they know.

So do the cows grazing in the fields, the walking paths lacing
through the woods, the ivy scaling oaks and telephone poles.

Even the manmade things—houses new and historical,
a meadow of solar panels, hissing high-tension lines—

they whisper as I pass, saying, *You are safe. This is not a dream.*
I want so badly to linger here, to pull over the car, curl up

among the roots or in a small cave, and hibernate until spring.
Instead, I reach the end of the street, exhale the drowsy ache

from my eyes, and know I'll be back tomorrow for more
of this street's lullaby until I remember how to sing my own again.

# Lament of the North Atlantic Right Whale

I didn't conceive a calf this year.
Nor did the other females in my pod.
If you could understand our language,
our moaning, pulsing songs,
you would know that every summer,
in the Bay of Fundy, we strain fewer and fewer
zooplankton and krill through the sieves of our mouths,
and not because our own numbers are growing.

My mother—
bless her shore-stranded soul—
once spoke of how these northern waters
used to be colder, cleaner, quieter.
Now, they're thick with sewage, oil, and fuel,
and congested with ships that slice the surface
like predators. They don't eat us,
but they've killed twenty of our kind
in the past two years with the knuckles of their hulls,
the spinning teeth of their propellers,
and the fingers of fishing nets
that scar our bodies.

My youngest child drowned in one
four springs ago. He wasn't even a year old
when he strayed too close to the boat
and the meshing slipped between his baleen plates.
I could only watch as he wrestled with the net;
as it ensnared his head and fins;
as blood streamed from the cuts in his storm-gray skin;
as, eventually, he stilled and closed his blowhole.

I've had no children since then,
and not for lack of trying.
Sometimes I imagine he's nudging my side
or, if I've rolled onto my back,
he's nestled between my flippers.
His weight was an ocean of comfort,
the callosities on his nose and jaw as beautiful
as the shimmer of moonlight through the sea at night.

There was another story my mother told me once:
how, many years ago, our unhurried pace
and coastal wanderings would catch the attention
of land-dwelling, harpoon-limbed hunters
who would later alchemize our deaths into gold
by boiling our blubber to harvest its oil.
Those pursuits have ended, as far as I've been told,
but sometimes I wonder
if we're still being hunted.

# The Spider

The spider knows what she is doing
when she picks the exact place
where she'll spin her web.
She builds her home herself
using her body and the silk she creates.
She needs no help, no instruction.

The spider does not hurry her construction.
She knows her work is painstaking, that it takes time
to form what will sustain her.
Her shelter, her invention, is a product
of her intuition, connecting her to branches, rafters,
blades of grass, and dead flowers.

The spider sees in many ways:
her eyes, the sensitive hairs on her legs,
the dainty plucking of strands on her web.
This helps her determine whether the fibers
need reinforcement, a potential mate has come to visit,
or a fly has been trapped for her next meal.

The spider means no harm. If you find her in
your house, invite her to stay and feed on
the flies that pester and the mosquitos that bite.
If she prefers your backyard, let her live there instead.
Her feet will not absorb pesticides into her
bloodstream, and she will crawl to a safer tree.

Whatever you do, do not remove the spider from your world.
If her kind were to vanish, other insect populations—
and their diseases—would multiply.
She cannot afford to be lost to legend, found only in
the stories of the weaver Arachne, the trickster Anansi,
or the Cherokee grandmother, the Lightbringer.

So when you see the spider on your wall
or the frame of her web on your porch,
ask yourself if it's necessary to kill her,
if it's necessary to wipe that corner clear
with a broom when you know
she will only come back to rebuild it.

# Glimpse of a Bald Eagle

I drive north on the Maine Turnpike,
just under the speed limit to avoid
puddles of ice and streaks of slush,
and in my peripheral vision
the world soars past,
pines and snow and rock blurring into
a fluvial black-and-white song of the season—

until a pair of eyes, gold like ripened wheat,
catch mine from the roadside,
and like a child I twist around in my seat,
quickly but not quick enough
so I catch only a glimpse of that stately body,
that head held high, half-camouflaged
in the white-brushed hillside,
that patriot's beak, that rippling robe
of dark brown feathers hiding the folds
of robust wings—

all hints that are just enough to tell me
who this bystander is,
enough so I don't confuse my bone-deep thrills
with the bumps in the winter-stricken road,
enough for me to press the memory to my chest
because a glimpse is never merely
a glimpse.

# Letter to Mother Earth During a Severe Drought

*Massachusetts, Summer 2022*

Earth under my feet, tell me:
Do you remember the last time it rained?
It's the middle of August, and since the spring equinox,
showers and thunderstorms have rolled through so rarely
that, when they do, the torrents,
the puddles, the slick pavement,
the pearls of moisture clinging to leaves
and daylily petals all seem like a mirage.
By day's end, the asphalt is once again a black desert,
and the ground is barely wet to the touch
because you've gulped down
every last drop.

When I step outside, even my eyes feel parched.
That is how thirsty you've become—
and I don't blame you. If I had no choice
but to drink only a drop of water each week
because that was all I was given,
I would hoard each deluge whenever it came.
I would be selective about who to share my windfall with,
even if it meant browning the grass to a crisp
and leaving the topsoil to bake into dust
just so the hydrangea blossoms could blush and purple,
just so this year's apples could swell with sweet flesh and juice,
just so I could live.

I need no reminders
that you are not the greedy one.
When I drive around town, sprinklers are spitting
and kiddie pools are overflowing despite the water ban,
as if we humans own this precious commodity
when, in reality, you need the relief more.

You need it so much that you've resorted
to swallowing rivers. It's breaking news now—
people are walking across shallows in the Loire in France,
the Po in Italy, the Danube in Romania,
the Charles here in Massachusetts.
Last night, while out for a walk,
I stopped at the brook limping past my street.
The water level was so low
that you were exposed—

a rise at the bottom of the brook's muddy bed,
surfacing like a whale before its breath geysers out.
But this was not an ocean, and you are not a whale,
and scientists say this may be the norm in the years to come:
summer after summer after hot, rainless summer,
until even the taps from our faucets
trickle to a crawl,
until those blessed

*drip*

*drip*

drips

are gone.

# An Ode to Icelandic Tap Water

I was told to drink you,
that you are "completely safe" and
"no other tap water on Earth tastes so good,"
and I cringed as if I had sipped rancid milk.
Where I come from, such water perfumes the skin
with trace metals during a shower,
and who knows what kind of slow death
it inflicts on one's cells.

Regardless, I pour my first glass of you,
and you appear as water should,
clear and cool to the touch.
What was I expecting?
Ale brewed by the sea giant Aegir?
Rain tapped from the heavens?
I honestly can't say, and so
I bring you to my lips—

and the earth pulls me down
through layers of lava rock and andisols
into the natural springs, where you come from.
You don't reek of iron, or taste of chlorine,
or leave flecks of residue on plastic containers
and liquid measuring cups,
or have the occasional misfortune
of being tainted with lead.

No. You smell of
sulfur, ozone, fresh-cut quartz.
You taste of basalt columns and cirrus clouds,
winter winds and spring cambium,
as if you tumbled out of a waterfall
and not from the faucet.

I drink you, and something ancient
seeps into my bloodstream,
cracks me open like a fissure
so I can listen to the earth, breathe in the glaciers,
and let the rust reds, the searing greens,
all the wildflower colors of this country kiss me.

Yes, my tongue is listening, and so am I.
Now that I've had a taste of you,
I want to bathe in you, imbibe you,
let you awaken me to everything
your sweet liquid mirror wants me to see.
I only hope that the next foreigner who meets you
does not waste or sully you,
but rather toasts to your clarity.

# Gifts

Why is it that, so often, we receive gifts
that we are not meant to keep?
Do we still thank the giver
for our wild and fleeting joy?
Do we steal the blessing home
and make space for it on a dusty shelf?
Yesterday I almost stepped on a turkey feather—
brown and white, slender and slightly curved,
longer than my forearm from shaft to tip.
I spun it between my fingers,
felt a slight give in the quill where it once
was joined with skin, and wondered
why it must hurt a bird so much
to molt this precious, deep-rooted part of itself
yet when we lose a strand of hair, we feel no pain.
So I gave the feather
back to the ground, where it belonged,
because no shelf, no picture frame,
no end table could replace
the warm and receptive cradle that is the earth,
because we have taken so much from the world
without permission
and now it is time to give something back.
Tell me, what would you have done
if you had stumbled upon such gold?
What will you do with that gift
if you know it can grace your hands
once and only once?

# Five

# At World's End

*Hingham, Massachusetts*

Have we come to the edge of the world?
It certainly seems so here, where the farthest path
follows the rim of the peninsula
before circling back toward the mainland;
where the wide, winding trail that beckoned us here
resembles a long-abandoned, tire-worn carriage road;
where a wall of oaks, maples, and catalpas shields us
from the Labor Day boat traffic in the harbor beyond
and we can drink up the peace that's encouraged
by the crisp shrilling of cicadas
and the crunching of grass underfoot.

It's the postcard image of an ending.
Yet, on today, my birthday, I stand only in beginnings:
a new year in the summer of my existence,
another year of sunlight warming my skin,
another year of living as verdantly
as drumlin meadows and full leaf canopies.
I look back at you now that we're standing in the shade,
then at our hands, fingers intertwined
like the limbs of the century-old sentinels surrounding us,
then back at the fence of trees just before the shore.
We could always turn around,
visit the rocky beach and the tidal marsh,
walk the other paths that weave through the park.
But the barrier ahead can't keep out
the salty heart-call of the sea
or hide the blue water that shimmers
through the gaps between their trunks,
and the burgeoning wild child in me thinks:

What if there was no edge of the world?
What if you and I—or anyone—
could defy the name of this sanctuary?
Would you come with me,
follow me if I tugged on your hand,
to see what lies on the other side?
Would you walk through that doorway
to the sky, the ocean, the future,
then find your footsteps quickening
until you're running because your blood
flows hot and blazing-bright like sunlight?
How far would you go?
What paths would you find?
Would it feel like heaven?
Or a little bit like home?
Let's find out, shall we?

# About the Author

Sara Letourneau is a poet as well as the editor, book coach, and writing workshop instructor at Heart of the Story Editorial & Coaching Services. She's also the cofounder of the Pour Me a Poem open mic in Mansfield, Massachusetts. Her poetry has won the Beals Prize for Poetry and the Blue Institute's 2020 Words on Water Contest and has appeared in Mass Poetry's *Poem of the Moment* and *Hard Work of Hope, Nixes Mate Review, Muddy River Poetry Review, The Avocet, Arlington Literary Journal, Constellations, Boston Area Small Press and Poetry Scene, Soul-Lit, Amethyst Review,* and *The Aurorean,* among others. *Wild Gardens* is her debut poetry collection and was shortlisted for Homebound Publications' 2023 Poetry Prize. She lives in Foxboro, Massachusetts.

Visit her online at:
heartofthestoryeditorial.com

www.ingramcontent.com/pod-product-compliance
Lightning Source LLC
Chambersburg PA
CBHW072202160426
43197CB00012B/2497